Betty Eve

52 Communication Tips

Weekly lessons for improving your relationships

2018

Arietta Press
Olympia, Washington

52 Communication Tips
Second Edition
By Betty Everitt Lochner

Published by Arietta Press
1827 Arietta Ave SE, Olympia, WA 98501

Ordering Information
Publications can be ordered direct from:
betty@cornerstone-ct.com

Quantity sales: special discounts are available on quantity purchases by organizations, associations, colleges and other groups.
52 Communication Tips is also available on Amazon.

ISBN-13: 978-1986822602
ISBN-10:1986822605

Cover photo by Carolyn Cummins, Shootinforfun.com

Edited by: Reyna Gobel

For Jerry Everitt, my dad and mentor.

1927-2018

INTRODUCTION

We all communicate constantly. Whether we think we are or not and whether we want to or not. We communicate by our words, or lack of words, by the body language we use, and by the intent we have. Learning how to communicate effectively in all situations is the most important area of self-development you can work on. It also pays the biggest dividends. Here's what research shows:

- A survey of employers found that the most **highly desired trait** in new recruits was **communication skills.**

- **80%** of employees who lost their jobs did so due to an **inability to communicate**. - The Carnegie Foundation

- **97.7%** of Fortune 500 vice presidents surveyed believe that **communication skills had affected their career advancement.**

- When CEO's from 5000 US companies were asked: *What are the three most important things you have learned in order to perform your role as an executive?* **They ranked communication as number one.**

The 52-week challenge

52 Communication Tips is a simple and powerful weekly study that focuses on helping you become more aware of how you communicate and how you can make small changes that will make a huge difference in all your relationships.

If you read and practice each short weekly tip, you will find yourself exploring several communication themes. Most lessons repeat in some way at least once over the course of the book. All lessons focus on the cornerstones of good communication – listening, building connections, and having positive relationships.

Do the exercises by yourself or as a work group trying to engage better with each other.

The Individual Challenge
Read one tip per week and work on that one short lesson. Always follow the lesson with an actionable goal you'd like to achieve.

Keep in mind that not everything you will learn in these lessons will be easy or right for you. In fact, not everything will work for your personality, your style, or your comfort level. It's okay to skip around or go back and do a lesson over. Just remember that usually whatever is most uncomfortable is what you most need to work on!

The Workplace Challenge
Use this book as part of team transformation by working on one tip together each week as part of a staff meeting or as a special 15-minute Monday morning meeting. When everyone is working on the same tip together, it provides accountability and the group engages in professional development together. It is a simple and powerful team building tool. Report successes at the next week's meeting.

Getting Started

Option 1: Get a notebook (or start an online document) and label it *My Communication Workbook* – or some other creative title. Take notes on each week's tip, review your previous week's work, and make a weekly personal action plan.

Option 2: Use this book as your workbook. Use the blank space at the end of each weekly tip to make notes on how you will put each tip into action.

Use whichever options works for you. The important part is to have a system for tracking your notes and progress. Then make a commitment to use it.

You do not have to work on these tips in order, though you may find it easier to do so to stay on track and not miss a week. These are also excellent tips and activities to do with someone else – for example, a spouse or co-worker.

Success Tips

- Starting today, pick a day each week that you will read a new communication tip. For each consecutive week, read a new lesson and work that lesson all week.

- Keep in mind that not everything learned in these lessons will be easy or right for you. It's okay to skip around or go back and do a lesson over.

- Be consistent and work on a new lesson each week, until you have completed all lessons you decided worked for your specific communication needs.

Table of Contents

TIP #1: Assess your communication skills.

Communication works for those who work at it. ~ John Powell

Every contact we make involves using communications skills. Speaking and listening, our attitude, speech patterns, the words we use, the tone of our voice, our body language and even the silences play a part in how successful our communications are.

To assess your current skills, answer each statement **True** or **False**.

1. I listen more than I talk.

2. I speak specifically and personally, instead of generally and abstractly.

3. My body language corresponds with my words and my tone.

4. I check my tone (especially in written communication) to make sure it corresponds with my message.

5. I pay attention to one person/conversation at a time.

6. I don't rely primarily on written (e-mail and text) conversations.

7. I am clear in what I am saying, and I share my expectations with others.

8. I make it comfortable or "safe" for others to talk to me about sensitive subjects.

9. I never avoid certain people or conversations. I tackle the hard conversations with ease.

10. I deal with issues as soon as they come up.

This week:

Make a list of the communication skills that you feel most confident with. What you are already doing well? Now, list the areas you identified in the self-assessment and any others that you want to work on in the upcoming weeks.

.

TIP #2: Become more self-aware.

Success means having the courage, the determination, and the will to become the person you believe you were meant to be. ~ George Sheehan

It's easy to spot what you don't like about how others communicate. However, how are you at knowing how **you** are coming across?

All of us can unintentionally convey messages that we don't mean. And, people can interpret our messages and habits in unexpected ways.

The easiest way to assess how well you are coming across is to enlist friends or family members who can assess whether you are communicating clearly or if you have some communication habits that need changing.

This week:

Ask a trusted friend or family member to give you specific feedback on your communication style. Make sure you are ready for the feedback. Pick someone who will be honest, yet kind.

Ask them to respond to the following:

- What do they like about how you communicate?
- What do they notice you could work on?

Ask them to share one to three things they notice that would make you a better communicator. What could you do more of, or less of?

Maybe it's talking too fast or interrupting. Maybe it's an excessive use of "ums", swallowing or fidgeting. Pay attention to what they share. Make sure you are open to the feedback without being defensive. Then, thank them for their feedback!

Pick just one thing you want to improve on and consciously work on that one thing each day this week. Soon, you'll see a new habit form and/or an old one go away.

TIP #3: Get comfortable with the uncomfortable.

Man's mind, once stretched by a new idea, never regains its original dimensions.
~ Oliver Wendell Holmes

We tend to repeat what we are comfortable doing. We often put off trying something new because it's out of our comfort zone. That is why, when it comes to communicating well, you need to work to do or say something that you aren't very comfortable with.

Think about the first time you spoke in front of a group or the first time you drove a car. You were probably nervous. Yet, by doing the activity, you were able to expand your comfort zone and learn a new skill. Each time you practice, you will perform the task with a higher level of competence and confidence than you had before.

It's the same with all new skills. Sometimes you just need to try it – even though it doesn't feel comfortable at first. The more you practice, the easier new skills will become. This is especially true with communication.

Soon the uncomfortable becomes comfortable.

This week:

Pick a communication challenge - something that you are nervous about doing or that's clearly out of your comfort zone. Maybe it's starting a conversation with your boss, asking for something you need someone to do, or admitting to someone that you were wrong.

Now, go out there and try it this week. No procrastinating allowed. Muster up some courage and just do it.

Assess how it went and write down your thoughts. Was it as hard as you thought it would be? How did it feel? Then learn from the experience and try it again. It will get easier each time.

TIP #4: Avoid the stuck state cycle.

If you do what you've always done, you will get what you've always gotten.
~ Tony Robbins, Author

When things are not going the way you want, do you keep repeating the same response or behavior but hope for or expect, something different to happen?

When that happens, it won't take long before you'll find yourself in a stuck state - repeating the same cycle over and over and getting the same result.

To get out of the stuck cycle, you must respond and react differently. Rather than responding to a situation in an unconscious and automatic way, try responding in a conscious and accountable way. You can do that by being **specific and clear** in stating what you want and why.

Let's say you repeatedly state that you need help on a project. You say it in the same way and the response you get back is always the same. Instead of continuing to ask in the same way with increasing anger, try asking in a new way.

For example, instead of an automatic response such as: "No one helped with the spreadsheet again," **say what you want and why.** Take a short pause and respond in a different and more accountable way. Try "In order to get this project done on time, I need help on the spreadsheet. Can you please help?"

This week:

List at least one situation at work or home that has you in a stuck state cycle. Think of a way to respond differently. Say what you want and why. Change the way and words used to ask for and describe what you need.

Think: What can I say or do to get a different response?

TIP #5: Shovel while your piles are small.

When we can no longer change a situation, we are challenged to change ourselves.
~ Viktor Frankl

Don't wait for a crisis to communicate. A small issue can turn into a really big one if you don't deal with it sooner rather than later.

The longer damaging or uncomfortable things are left unspoken, the longer they remain damaging and uncomfortable and the bigger the pile gets, until one day – Kaboom! Now you have a really big issue or problem to deal with.

Rather than avoiding issues that come up - or hoping they will go away - address them soon after they happen. Don't wait.

Here's how: Have the conversation you need to have the first time the issue comes up in a kind and respectful way.

For example, if something happens that just doesn't feel right, instead of letting it go, address it. For example, "It seems like you aren't happy with me. Can we talk about that?", or, "Can you help me understand the problem and how I can help fix it?" or "I'm concerned that this is happening. Can we talk about how to resolve it?"

Speak your truth sooner rather than later and mind your piles.

This week:

Identify an issue in your life that you need to deal with. Most of us can think of several. Maybe it's the neighbor's dog messing in your yard. Maybe it's a disagreement at work.

Think through or talk with someone about how you should deal with it. Practice saying what you will say and how you will say it. Remember, being kind and respectful is key to addressing issues.

Write about what pile you are going to shovel this week. What is your plan? Now – go deal with it!

TIP #6: Beware of distractions.

An empty stomach will not listen to anything. ~ Spanish Proverb

Do you ever get distracted and have no idea what the person talking to you just said?

How many times have you been interrupted, changed your focus for a minute and then thought: "Now where was I?"

As technology allows people to do more tasks at the same time, living the myth that we can multi-task has never been stronger. However, researchers say it's still a myth — and there is plenty of data to prove it.

Humans do not have the ability to do more than one thing simultaneously.

Instead, we must switch our attention from task to task extremely quickly. People that appear to be good multi-taskers simply have a very good memory as they switch back and forth.

In our busy world, we are constantly tempted to multi-task. The results can wreak havoc on our communication with someone else.

When you text, type, take a phone call, or do some other task while you are communicating with someone, you are telling them "I don't really care" and "I'm not really listening to you."

And, really, you aren't.

This week:

Focus only on the one conversation you are having. Don't check your watch or look away, fidget with small objects, text, or multi-task in any way.

Is it harder than you thought it would be to stay focused on just the conversation? Write about your experience. What area do you need the most work on?

Practice improving on that one thing every day this week.

TIP #7: Slow your listening down.

The first step to wisdom is silence; the second is listening. ~ Carl Summer

All good communication begins with good listening.

The problem is that most of us don't listen very well. For most of us, listening doesn't come naturally. In fact, recent surveys show that less than 2% of people have had formal training in listening. That means 98% of us could use some help.

We speak an average of 120 words per minute, but listen four times faster. Our minds fill the gap by thinking of other things and wandering off.

Which of the following have you ever thought about (be honest) while someone is talking to you?

- *Get to the point.*
- *I already know what you are going to say. I'm way ahead.*
- *This is boring, I'm checking out.*
- *What should I have for dinner?*
- *How should I respond?*
- *How can I defend my position?*

If you thought of something even close to any of the above when you should be listening, you need to make a choice to really listen to understand what is being said. Stay focused. Slow down your listening and **listen more than you talk.**

This week

Pick at least one conversation each day where you concentrate solely on listening. Be fully aware and present in the moment. Avoid distractions and listen as if what you are hearing could change your life. Just be still and *listen*. Don't interrupt, **ask** clarifying questions, and summarize what you hear as appropriate. Simple, but hard to master.

Write down how you perceive yourself as a listener. Do you need practice listening? How might you do that?

Practice listening in every conversation you have this week.

TIP #8: Know your body language.

When we seek to bring out the best in others, we bring out the best in ourselves.
~ William Arthur

Your body language says a lot about you. Experts say it makes up over 70% of your total communication message. That leaves only 30% of our communication to the words you use.

To be an effective communicator, your body language should help you connect and engage.

Here are three important body language basics:

1) Look up and make level eye contact.

   Maintain eye contact and whenever possible be on the same level as the person you are talking to. If they are standing, then stand. If they are sitting, then sit. This creates a positive and neutral connection.

2) Keep your body posture open.

   When you put your hands on your hips, it can be interpreted as a sign of superiority, arrogance, or defensiveness. Crossing your arms can show anger or superiority, or that you are "closed". For best results, try to keep your arms open and at your sides or use small hand movements to make a point.

3) Nod and smile: show some positive (and genuine) signs that you are listening!

Mastering the use of good body language will make a huge difference in the connection you make and the success of your communication.

This week:

In each conversation you have this week, be aware of what your body is doing. Maintain appropriate eye contact, get on their level, stay engaged, keep your arms by your side, and show that you are paying attention.

Write about what you learned about your body language. Do these subtle changes work for you?

TIP #9: Be succinct.

The more the words, the less the meaning, and how does that profit anyone?
~ Ecclesiastes 6:11

If you want someone to understand and remember what you are saying, you need to keep your message simple and stick to making only a few major points. The more succinct your message is, the more likely you are to get your points across.

- Don't try to make more than three-five points at a time.
  If you make this a habit when you are giving a presentation, sharing information, or trying to persuade someone to see your point of view, you will improve your chances that your message will be heard and remembered.

- Keep your message uncomplicated and use simple language.
  Stay away from technical terms, unnecessarily big or academic words, jargon, and acronyms as much as you can.

This week:

Take an opportunity each day to make your point in as few words as possible. Work on keeping your communication straight-forward and simple. Think about the words you choose, and don't make your message too complicated.

Don't repeat yourself or go on and on when a few words suffice.

Write down how that worked for you. Is this an area you need more work on, or are you fairly confident that you communicate in a succinct way on a regular basis? If you aren't sure, ask a trusted friend or colleague. Then, make some adjustments.

TIP #10: Listen actively.

Be a good listener. Unlike your mouth, your ears will never get you in trouble. ~
Frank Tyger

The best communicators are also the best listeners. That's why we are
going to spend more time on building (see tip #7) on your listening
skills this week.

Becoming an active listener means that you make a conscious effort to
truly hear what the other person is saying – by paying attention to their
words as well as their body language.

Here are a few important active listening tips:

1) Practice holding off thinking about how to respond until you
   have thoroughly heard what they are saying.
2) Do not allow yourself to be distracted.
3) Make appropriate eye contact with the speaker.
4) Show you are listening by nodding.
5) Don't interrupt. Allow the speaker to finish making his point.
6) Say, "tell me more".
7) Ask questions for clarification to make sure you understand.
8) Summarize what you heard.
9) Ask if you understood correctly.

Active listening shows respect and engagement and will increase your
success at understanding the message intended.

This week:

Rate in order how well you do the 9 listening tips from 1-9, with 1 being the one you are most comfortable doing. Now, work on the ones with higher numbers. Use these tips in each conversation you have.

TIP #11: Build your appreciation muscle.

You shouldn't say 'I love you' unless you really mean it. Then you should say it a lot.
People forget that. ~ Jessica, Age 8

Appreciation ~ The act of noticing and recognizing the people around you in a positive way

Everyone has a basic need to feel appreciated and valued. In fact, a study at the University of Washington found that in healthy relationships positive to negative comments should be at a ratio of 9:1. But, the opposite is true. In most relationships, the positive to negative comments are 1:10. For every positive comment we give, we give 10 negative comments. We live in a culture that is starved for appreciation.

Showing genuine appreciation is one of the most powerful communication tools you can develop. It will open doors to a better conversation, a more positive exchange, and ultimately a better relationship.

A note about receiving appreciation: When someone tells you something they appreciate about you, simply answer "thank you". Give them the courtesy of accepting their appreciation. Don't disagree or make excuses ("oh, this old thing?"). Don't contribute to making it hard or uncomfortable for people to appreciate you. Simply accept it with grace.

This week:

Appreciation is like a muscle. You need to use it to make it stronger.

Go out of your way to appreciate someone. Give a compliment or tell someone they are doing a good job. Be specific, look them in the eye and tell them what you appreciate about them.

Write about how it felt to actively appreciate daily. Was it hard or uncomfortable? Does it get easier? Can you see the immediate results?

TIP #12: Build rapport.

The secret of success is not very hard to figure out. The better you are at connecting with other people, the better the quality of your life. ~ Nicholas Boothman, Author

People connect to people that they feel comfortable with. One way to build rapport is to behave and talk in similar patterns, even choosing the same or similar words that the person you are talking to uses. Learning to build good rapport with someone isn't hard and can even be a lot of fun. Here's how to do it:

1) **Choose your attitude.** Your attitude always precedes you, especially in a face-to-face interaction. Begin the interaction with a smile, an open mind, a positive attitude, and make it **YOUR** responsibility to connect.

2) **Observe the other person's behavior.** Watch their mannerisms – how they sit, how fast they talk, whether they lean in, talk with their hands, shuffle their feet, etc.

3) **Mimic the body language you've observed.** Deliberately, but subtly, alter your behavior for a short time. Adapt to their mannerisms and communication style. If they are leaning in, lean in. If they are smiling, smile back. Mimic, in a subtle way, their mannerisms. Match their vocal tone and speed.

4) **Listen.** Practice your active listening skills (see tip #10), the most powerful connector of all.

This week:

Find at least one person that you want to connect with each day and subtly mimic their body language. Don't overdo it, and work on connecting through making similar movements, vocal tone, and speed.

Write down what worked and what didn't. Can you see a difference in the rapport you created?

TIP #13: Pause.

It takes two people to speak the truth - one to speak and one to listen.
~ Henry David Thoreau

Here's one of my best tips for avoiding a communication problem. It's called **PAUSE!**

Pausing is more than just a moment in time. It requires us to become quiet inside and allow our internal resources to assist us in how we should respond. It means thinking first before speaking.

Pausing can save us a lot of headaches. In most cases it will help with your pile prevention (see tip #5).

When you consciously pause, you will automatically help slow your listening down. Using a pause is a trigger you give yourself to listen first and **then** respond in a conscious and non-automatic way. It's a choice you can make each time you communicate with someone.

Since our natural instinct is to immediately do or say something, the simplicity of a pause isn't always easy.

This week:

In at least one conversation each day consciously take a pause and listen first. Use the power of a pause to improve your conversations.

Write about how your pausing is going. Is it easy or difficult? What differences do you see when you consciously pause?

Some of us naturally are better at pausing than others, and some of us – well, we may need to come up with a pause reminder – maybe a sticky note on your desk or frig, or a screen saver on your computer as a reminder to consistently PAUSE!

TIP #14: Know who you are talking to.

I've learned that people will forget what you said, people will forget what you did, but people will never forget how you made them feel. - Maya Angelou

To effectively communicate, we must realize that we are all different in the way we perceive the world. Most people don't intentionally try to frustrate or disappoint us. Their behavior is partly based on the values and characteristics they bring from their generational, gender, or cultural perspective.

No matter how we categorize personalities, behaviors, or communication styles, everyone is unique. It is for many different reasons that we don't all communicate in the same way.

To be an effective communicator, you must be able to observe and consider all differences when you are communicating with others. Be responsive to your differences. Think from the perspective of the person you are talking to and put yourself in their shoes.

You will find that you have more in common with each other than you think.

This week:

Find one person from another generation, culture, or behavioral style and engage in a conversation. Listen and don't judge their appearance or anything that strikes you as different. Let go of any biases you have. Listen and try to really see their point of view.

Write down your experience – how did it go?

TIP #15: Learn someone's story.

I am a part of all that I have met. ~ Alfred Tennyson

Everyone has a story. When you learn the stories of those around you, you become more compassionate and can see the world from their perspectives.

When you can connect personally with someone, you are more likely to understand and even appreciate their perspective.

When you are communicating with someone, try to understand where they are coming from:

- Ask open-ended questions to get them to tell you some of their personal story, such as what they like to do, what their family and work background is, etc.

- What do you have in common? Who are they? What were their experiences?

Keep digging until you find something you have in common. It can be something very simple. For example, do you have the same color or type of purse, bag, or other personal item? Do you notice they have small children too? How about hobbies or pets? Do you live in the same area of town?

Work to find something in common that you can both relate to. Then use it to make a personal connection.

Creating a personal connection will ultimately lead to better communication.

This week:

Pick at least one person you work with that you don't know very well. Ask questions, show interest in learning about them, and find your common connection. What was it?

TIP #16: Take a tech break.

The single biggest problem in communication is the illusion that it has taken place.
~ George Bernard Shaw

Do you ever use email or text to avoid having a face-to-face conversation?

Living in our fast-paced world of texting and constant conversation can short-change your relationships and get in the way of clear, effective, and meaningful communication.

More and more of our daily communication is done via email, voicemail, and text messaging. There are advantages and disadvantages to each of these, depending on the message and the audience. For example, texting can be effective when a quick question or answer is required without further explanation or repeated follow-up.

However, while using technology to communicate can be a useful tool for exchanging quick information, it can also get in the way of communicating well. A good rule of thumb is: **Only text or email when it's a simple message, transactional, or you need a short, quick response.**

When you call or talk to someone in person, you are showing that you care enough to have a real-life conversation with them, without abbreviations and instead of doing something else at the same time. You choose to focus just on them. And, focusing only on communicating well will make a huge difference in how well you understand and are understood.

This week:

Take a break from constant use of technology to communicate. Resist the urge to text or email when it's more appropriate to have a conversation by phone or face-to-face.
At least once each day, take the initiative to pick up the phone and start with, "Hello - It's so nice to hear your voice." Better yet, have the conversation in person.

Write down how it goes. Are you more addicted to technology than you thought?

TIP #17: Don't assume.

Some things I'll never change, but 'til I try I'll never know.
~ Elphaba, from the musical *Wicked*

Most of us don't say what we really want. We want others to do what we want them to do even though we don't tell them what that is. No wonder we have so much trouble being heard and understood.

Even if you know someone well, be careful not to assume you know what they want or need. Don't make assumptions or play the mind reader game. Ask questions and then check for understanding.

For example, don't assume because you like pizza on Fridays that others do. Ask first. Share what's on your mind and ask others to do the same.

Moving from being a passive communicator to a more assertive communicator is strength, not a weakness. Being honest and digging for what is really being asked is a skill that will move you out of the assumption trap and into real and honest communication.

This week:

Write down examples of conversations that you made assumptions without asking for clarifying details. Work on asking questions to make sure you understand what someone wants or needs.

TIP #18: Make your expectations clear.

Whatever we expect with confidence becomes our own self-fulfilling prophecy.
~ Brian Tracy, Author

People want to know what you expect of them. People will almost always try to meet your expectations if you just tell them what they are.

Be clear from the beginning about what you expect about behavior, performance, appearance, deadlines, and processes. Don't expect people around you to be mind readers. Instead, communicate clearly what you want.

Be certain that the information you need to convey – whether it is written or spoken – is clear and directly communicated. Use language that is specific and unambiguous. Check that the receiver understands the message as you intended. Avoid acronyms when there's a chance they will be unclear.

Here is an example of how to communicate expectations,
> Here is what I expect:
>> Here's what that looks like?
>> Do you understand?
>> Can you do that?

Be open and honest about your expectations and give respectful feedback when you get behavior you didn't expect or that isn't appropriate for the situation.

Don't assume that people understand your undisclosed expectations! For example, don't roll your eyes when the skirt is too short. Instead, simple say: "that skirt is too short for our workplace. " State specifically what you need and want.

This skill will solve most, if not all, of your workplace problems.

This week:

Practice being clear and telling people what you expect and want. Have a conversation that starts with "I would like you to" or "I want this to happen." When you catch yourself not being clear; start over.

Be specific and state your expectations right up front. Don't wait until someone disappoints you because they didn't know what you expected.

TIP #19: Say please and thank you.

God gave you a gift of 86,400 seconds today.
Have you used one to say "thank you"?
~ -William A. Ward

This should be an easy one – but most people are please and thank you deficient. In fact, you may overestimate how well you are consistent in this area of communication. It's important, yet easy to neglect.

Make it a habit to ALWAYS say please and thank you to everyone in your path. It not only shows respect but also sets the stage for positive and effective communication.

Be consistent. Say please and thank you to the grocery clerk, your kids, your co-workers, everyone you come in contact with every day. If you are sincere and genuine when you are speaking you really can't overdo this tip.

This week:

Practice saying "please" and "thank you" each day to everyone you encounter. Overuse it and make it a good communication habit. Keep a daily count of how many times you had to remind yourself. You may be surprised by how many times we can catch ourselves not saying please and thank you.

TIP #20: Smile more.

Of all the things you wear, your expression is the most important. ~ Janet Lane

Studies show you have only 90 seconds to make a good first impression.

Smiling is one of the easiest, and best things you can do to make a positive first impression. And, a positive first impression sets the stage for good communication.

A genuine smile wrinkles the corners of your eyes and changes the expression of your entire face. Fake smiles only involve the mouth and lips. You can also hear a smile over the phone in your voice.

A smile can be seen as far as 30 feet away, so don't wait until you are face-to-face, start that smile early.

This week:

Each time you are in a new situation and every time you enter a room, make an effort to smile genuinely. Actively turn a neutral or frowning expression into a smile. You will prepare the setting for open and positive communication.

Write about your smiling experience. Did you catch yourself frowning more than you thought you would?

TIP #21: Make gratitude a habit.

It's important to make gratitude a habit because your habits create your life.
~ Sandy Harper, author

Gratitude is the act of being thankful. While appreciation focuses on what you appreciate about someone, gratitude is the act of **being thankful** for what they have contributed to your life and for the blessings that they bring into your life.

Making gratitude a daily habit will set the tone for your day, every day. It will help you recognize what is important in your life and help you put things in perspective. This alone will have a huge impact on how you communicate and present yourself to others.

Being grateful for what and who you have in your life helps toward developing a positive outlook. Therefore, becoming a more positive communicator.

If you practice gratitude daily, the results in your life will be transforming.

This week:

Keep a daily gratitude journal. At the beginning of each day, take just a few minutes to write down everything that you are thankful for in your life. It can be for the people you love, or it can be as simple as having hot water for a shower and food in your cupboard. Starting your day with this act of gratitude, will prepare you to be receptive and grateful for everything your day will bring.

TIP #22: Seek out good work.

Kind words can be short and easy to speak but their echoes are truly endless.
~ Mother Teresa

Most people notice when something is not going well – when someone does something wrong. But, do you ever go out of your way to catch someone doing something **right?**

This tip is a small thing that will make a huge difference in developing positive communication. **Catch someone doing something right and then recognize them for it.** Do it as soon as you catch them. The sooner you do it, the more effective the feedback is.

For example, say something positive right away when someone picks up something that has fallen down, helps you on a project, or cleans your dishes in the sink.

Telling someone specifically what they did that you liked or appreciated. Reinforcing good behavior will encourage good work to continue. Catching someone doing something right is a huge motivator and takes a big step toward practicing positive communication.

Be on the lookout for good things going on around you. Then, when you see good work, recognize it.

This week:

Find at least one person each day that is doing something right. Seek them out and tell them right away. It will make both of you feel good. Write down who you selected and what you said.

TIP #23: Be tough and tender.

Whenever you're in conflict with someone, there is one factor that can make the difference between damaging your relationship and deepening it. That factor is attitude. ~ William James

When you find yourself in a potential conflict situation, or find yourself in a difficult conversation with someone, make sure you focus on the issue at hand and not the person.

Be careful not to blame or accuse. Instead, describe the actions or behavior that caused the conflict or stress between the two of you. Say something like, "I'm sensing that there are some issues between the two of us that we need to talk through." or "I'm feeling that I might have done something to upset you. Can we talk about it?"

Work on changing what people do, not who they are, by focusing on what the issue or problem is. Then, be tender (that means be kind and respectful) to the person.

For example, "I appreciate the hard work you've been doing on this project. However, we talked about arriving at work on time and the for past two days you have been over 20 minutes late. We need to come up with a way for you to be here on time every day. What can you do differently tomorrow to make that happen?"

This week:

Practice having at least one conversation where you focus specifically on the problem behavior or issue at hand while being tender with the person. Focus on the specific behavior or issue at hand and describe what you want to have happen. Write about your experience.

TIP #24: It's all in a name.

I always have trouble remembering three things: faces, names, and I can't remember what the third thing is. ~ Fred Allen

Studies show that a person's first name is their favorite word to hear. So, it makes sense that you will connect with someone more if you remember and use their name. People love the sound of their name and will stay better focused on YOU and what YOU have to say.

But, for many of us, remembering names is a challenge. Here are a few techniques you can try. The first is don't tell yourself you can't remember names. That just trains your brain to believe that and it will most certainly become a self-fulfilling prophecy. Instead, tell yourself that you *can* remember names. Your brain will work on that message instead.

Here are three more tips:

1) When you meet someone, or see someone whose name you want to remember, repeat his or her name immediately. Then, use it three times right away. Example – "Nice to meet you, Betty"; "Are you new to this group, Betty?" "Betty, I'd like you to meet Joe." It will feel awkward but do it anyway.

2) Associate the person whose name you want to remember with something. Say the person's name and make a descriptive statement about it out loud. For example, say something like: "Betty, I you're your red coat. It matches your hair color." This gives your brain more data to sort and store, making retrieval easier at a later date. The longer your brain gets to process the information you are giving it, as in giving more details and specifics, the better.

3) Try rhyming. For example: "Betty, rhymes with Freddie, who is my next door neighbor." Again, this gives your brain a chance to work for you, putting information together that will later give you some clues to help you remember. Don't necessarily say rhymes like this out loud.

This week:

Pick out one person each day, whose name you don't know or remember and find a way to remember it. Use the memory tips here and see how you do. And, once you have the name figured out — use it every time you see that person.

TIP #25: Check for understanding.

To know is not to know, unless someone else has known that I know.
~ Lucillius (B.C. 148-103)

Listen first. Then, ask open-ended questions to get more information and to clarify your understanding. Open-ended questions are questions that are not answered with yes or no. Asking open-ended questions will help you understand what the person is really trying to communicate.

Focus on trying to learn the facts, their feelings, and their perceptions of the situation or issue.

Consider asking these questions:
>What happened next?
>How do you feel about that?
>Why do you think that?

If you still don't understand, say "please help me understand," or "tell me more." Sometimes you may need to ask using different words. For example, if they say something like, "the thing didn't work, and it's just not fair." You may want to ask them to use a different word for thing.

Once you have gotten the facts, feeling and perceptions, summarize in your own words what you heard and confirm your understanding.

This week:

See if you can catch yourself asking a closed-ended (yes/no) question and switch to an open-ended one. Practice the habit of always checking to make sure you understand by getting to the facts, feelings and perceptions.

TIP #26: Choose positive words.

One of the best ways to persuade others is with your ears - by listening to them.
~ Dean Rusk, former Secretary of State

Changing the words you use and the connotations they have can make a huge difference in how the conversation goes. Here are some small and easy word choices you can use to make your language more positive and inclusive.

- **I Understand** - When you respond with "I understand," you will disarm 80% of any negative or resistant energy. Those two words make people feel heard and understood and will pave the way for better communication.

If you don't understand, say, "Can you clarify that for me just a little bit more?"

- **Replace "But" with "And"** - To avoid making someone feel like you are negating what they are saying, try replacing but with and. **But** acts as a stop word, and the other person stops listening. Instead of "Yeah, I hear what you're saying, *"but ..."*, try, "Yeah, I hear what you're saying, *and* here's something else I was thinking about in addition to that."

- Use **"We" more often**- Using we instead of I or You is a way to help us to connect and identify with others. This can avoid making the other person feel like must they're being singled out or criticized. Instead of saying, "You have a way to go," say, "**We** have a way to go."

Learning to choose different, more inclusive words takes a little bit of practice. Pay attention to what you are saying and make some simple word changes for better communication results.

This week:

Think about the words you choose. Work on choosing positive, inclusive words. Practice some of the examples listed on the previous page and use them in your day-to-day conversations.

TIP #27: Listen up.

Don't judge each day by the harvest you reap, but by the seeds you plant.
~ Robert Louis Stevenson

Active listening takes our whole attention and focus. When we make that effort, the rewards are huge: happier marriages and families, better communication at work, fewer misunderstandings between friends and others, and calmer, less stressful lives.

Take this quick listening assessment to see how you are doing so far:

1. *Listening means paying attention.*
   When I listen to someone, I focus my attention on the speaker. I look directly at him or her and concentrate on hearing what he or she is saying.
   __Always __ Most of the time __Sometimes __Never

2. *Listening means accepting what the other person says.*
   When I listen to someone, I withhold judgment and accept what he or she is saying as is. I acknowledge what the person is saying without labeling it right or wrong, good or bad, or true or false.
   __Always __ Most of the time __Sometimes __Never

3. *Listening means being interested in what the other person says.*
   When I listen to someone, I invite the speaker to give his or her opinion, say what's on his or her mind, or say how he or she feels about the topic or issue.
   __Always __ Most of the time __Sometimes __Never

Listening bonus: when you listen well, you become someone other people want to listen to.

This week:

Do you need to work on any of the three listening focus areas? Which ones are they? How will you improve?

TIP #28: Ask for what you want.

Words are the most powerful drug used by mankind. ~ Rudyard Kipling

Asking for what you want is a powerful and empowering act that has a ripple effect through all areas of your life.

To ask for and receive what you want, make sure four things are in place:

1. Decide what you want. People won't be able to figure it out if you don't even know.

2. Believe you deserve it. Don't doubt yourself. If you ask for something yet don't believe you deserve it, you won't be happy with any result.

3. You are prepared to accept no as an answer. Sometimes, the answer will be no, yet that should not be a reason for not asking.

4. You have the communication skills needed for an effective request. Be confident, direct and have the courage to ask in a clear and direct way.

This Week:

Have the courage to ask, and then follow the four steps. You won't know the answer if you don't ask. And, you may be amazed at what you'll get.

TIP #29: Be positive.

Be happy in the moment, that's all.
Each moment is all we need, not more. ~ Mother Theresa

Are you glass is half full or the glass is half empty kind of person? The truth is, some of us need to work on being the spreader of joy rather than the pessimist of the office or family.

When you are positive, it is harder for others around you to be negative. You can make a huge impact by simply being positive.

Always bring your best self to work. If you are struggling with issues at home, leave them at home and look for the positive in everything you do.

This week:

Think about how you come across. Are you the grumpy one that is never satisfied? Or are you the one people want to be around and talk to because you love life and it shows?

What can you do this week to be an even more positive influence on those around you?

TIP #30: Give feedback.

When we seek to discover the best in others, we bring out the best in ourselves. ~ William Arthur

Feedback is an important element of communicating well. Giving constructive feedback can change behaviors and allow you to share important information.

First, ask "Can I give you some feedback?" If the answer is yes (which it almost always is), then use the tips below. Note: if they say "no," wait. They are telling you that they aren't ready or for receiving feedback.

Follow these tips for giving effective feedback:

- **Identify and share you want to have happen next.** Be specific and clear.

- **what Clarify your intentions.** Identify right up front what you want to address.

- **Keep the feedback tailored to the individual** - not a group, or by association, but just that one person's behavior.

- **Give feedback close to the event.** Feedback loses its impact the longer you wait. What's important to you may be forgotten by someone else if you wait.

- **Describe specifically what you observed.** Give examples.

- **Focus on the behavior and not the person.** Address specific behavior you want changed, not what you don't like about the person.

- **Pause and check for understanding**. Make sure you are understood by asking questions.

This week:

Do you have some feedback you need to give? Use the feedback tips with at least one person this week.

TIP #31: Assess first.

The road to success is always under construction. ~ Lily Tomlin

Many times we jump to try to resolve a conflict when we really need to answer this*: Should I even have this conversation?*

To help you think through your decision of whether you need to have a hard conversation in the first place, here are some questions you can ask yourself *before* you react.

Think of a conversation that you think may need to happen or review one you've had lately. Write down your answers to the following questions:

1) **Why do I think I should have this conversation?** What do you want to gain from having this conversation? It is important enough to go to bat for what is important to you?

2) **What is the worst that could happen if I have this conversation?** Think through the worse-case scenarios of addressing this issue. Could you ruin a family event? Lose a friend? Make a landlord mad at you? Make the situation worse? Be as specific as you can and weigh out the risks if things don't go the way you plan.

3) **What is the best that could happen if I address this issue?** What do you hope will happen? What would be the absolute best solution to this problem? Is there a solution to this problem?

4) **What if I do nothing?** If this conversation doesn't happen, what are the consequences? Are they worth risking? Does it really matter? If you decide not to have the conversation, be prepared to let it go and move on.

6) **If I decide I need to have this conversation, how can I do it well?** Think about what you need to say and how to say it. Always practice first. Don't be unprepared!

This week:

When you see a conflict coming, ask yourself, "do I really need to have this conversation?"

Then decide, thoughtfully, if and how you will have it. If you decide to have the conversation, use your skills and have the courage to handle it well.

TIP #32: Validate someone.

When women say, 'Do I look fat in this?' they're asking for some deeper validation. It's not about fashion advice. ~ Jessica Weiner

val·i·date [val-i-deyt] - to make valid; substantiate; confirm - like when we get our ticket validated for free parking.

To validate someone is to confirm, to them, that they have worth and that they play an important role. A validation is usually an observation that is general in nature. For example, recognizing they are thoughtful, kind, beautiful, or good at what they do.

When you validate someone for something they do for you that makes your life better or easier, you show them a very affirming and confirming type of appreciation.

For example, validate someone when they retrieve coffee when you've left it lying somewhere, when a neighbor smiles when you walk by, or when your officemate offers to help with a project.

To validate someone:

- Start with the description of what they are doing and confirm it in a general statement.

    Some examples: "You are so thoughtful to bring my coffee to me.", "You are always so helpful.""You are so kind to me.", or "You're so great at your job."

It feels good to be validated.

This week:

Find one person to validate each day for something they have done to make your day better . Start the validation with "you are so....," or "you always...."

TIP #33: Describe the gap.

Expect the best of yourself, and then do what is necessary to make it a reality.
~ Ralph Marston

An effective way to give constructive feedback is to simply **describe the gap**.
When you are in a situation where something doesn't go the way you expected it to, describing the gap is a simple way to give constructive feedback and help resolve the problem.

Here are the steps you use in describing the gap:

Say,
1. We have a problem – and I need your help.

2. Here is what I was expecting... (explain what your expectations were)

3. Here is what I was experiencing... (explain what happened that was different than the expectations).

4. We need to close the gap between those two points. What can we do differently?

For example, "Here's what we talked about and what I expected, and here's what I saw happen. That isn't what we talked about. How can we work on fixing the gap between what we agreed to and what really happened? What will you do differently next time?"

This week:

Try describing the gap when you have a situation where you got something different from someone than expected.

TIP #34: Paraphrase.

The greatest compliment that was ever paid me was when someone asked me what I thought and attended to my answer. ~ Henry David Thoreau

Paraphrasing is simply repeating in your own words what has been said to make sure that you understand.

The goals of paraphrasing are to:

1) Make sure you are clear about what has been said.

2) Let the speaker know that you understand what he or she is communicating.

Both are equally important in effective communication.

Try this paraphrasing technique: "What I hear you saying is…" or "So you are saying that…" or "It sounds like…"

Then check for understanding. Say, "Is that right?" or "Is that what you are saying?"

You may be surprised at first at how many times you thought you understood what was being said but learned differently after you paraphrased the message back.

This week:

Practice paraphrasing to make sure you understand what you heard is what was said. Before you respond, repeat in your own words what you heard.

TIP #35: Be patient.

Patience is also a form of action. ~ Auguste Rodin

Sometimes people say things that are hurtful or that disappoint or frustrate us. When that happens, what do you do? For most of us, when our emotions are tapped in a negative way, our first reaction is to become angry and react as such.

When emotions are running high, it is better to hold your tongue than to say something you may later regret. That means you must learn the skill of being patient.

Being patience can mean that you do at least one of the following:
- Pause before responding (see Tip #13).

- Take a time out to think about how you will respond.

- Practice your response.

When you choose to be patient, you respond in a positive way to a negative situation. Patience brings an internal calm to an external storm.

Being patient helps you make a choice of whether you control your emotions or you let your emotions control you.

This week:

The next time someone says something hurtful or frustrating to you, pause first, then practice responding without being negative. If you cannot do that, then choose to say nothing at all. Write about how easy or difficult that is for you. How well are you at showing patience when emotions are running high?

TIP #36: Kindness counts.

In this life, we cannot always do great things. But we can do small things with great love.
~ Mother Teresa

Another way to display an attitude of open and positive communication is to practice being kind to others.

Kindness and compassion are a few of the basic things that make our lives meaningful. Showing kindness is a valuable communication skill – kindness connects us.

For those who have ever wondered whether tiny acts of kindness have larger consequences, researchers have shown that generosity really is contagious.

A series of studies on the influence of the behavior of kindness found that acts of giving were tripled over the course of the experiment when people saw others being kind and generous. It's the classic monkey see, monkey do response. The study found that when people were generous, even when it seemed irrational, others followed suit.

So, go out there and be kind. A single act of kindness can influence dozens more.

This week:

Catch yourself when you are behaving in a way that is anything but kind, regardless of the situation. Then change your behavior.

TIP #37: Make it safe.

They say time changes things, but you actually have to change them yourself. ~
Andy Warhol

When people feel safe talking to you, they can be open, honest and real. To feel safe, people need to have the confidence that you are open to hearing them without judgement or criticism. They must also know that you will honor your relationship by listening confidentially.

Here are five ways to cultivate a safe environment for open communication:

1. **Be approachable.** Have an open-door policy at work and at home. Don't just say you are approachable, be approachable. Invite people in and have a welcoming environment.

2. **Listen without judging.** Always use your active listening skills. Refrain from responding until absolutely necessary.

3. **Display an attitude of discovery and curiosity.** Be interested and engaging. Ask questions. Stay focused and avoid distractions.

4. **Provide regular positive feedback.** Look for the good and don't focus on the bad. Always start with something positive, even if you have something else you need to talk about.

5. **Give feedback in a kind, respectful, and timely way.** Follow the tools for providing feedback (Tip #30).

When there is enough safety in a relationship, anything can be discussed.

This week:

Do you provide a safe environment in which others can share what they are thinking, feeling and wanting?

Write about what you can do to improve making a safe environment for others to talk to you about anything.

TIP #38: Be Courageous.

Courage doesn't always roar. Sometimes courage is the quiet noise at the end of the day saying, I will try again tomorrow. ~ Mary Anne Radmacher

For many of us, we are afraid of taking a risk, of being embarrassed, or of making a mistake. We hang back and don't do or say what we need to in a timely manner.

Becoming a more skilled communicator includes learning to be more courageous. It means getting out of your comfort zone. It also means sometimes failing and trying again.

It takes courage to look beyond your own point of view and to try to see things as the other person does. It also takes courage to admit to being wrong.

Don't be afraid to try something new and to practice or improve on your communication skills. You will find that if you can muster up the courage to have the conversation you need to have, you could be more successful than you could have hoped.

Even if things don't go as well as you would like, you will have made one more step towards gaining confidence to try again.

If the conversation doesn't go well, admit it and start over. Say: "That's not how I wanted this to happen." or "That's not what I meant to say." or "I'm sorry."

This Week:

Have a courageous conversation you need to have. Write about how it went.

TIP #39: Have positive intent.

Be a rainbow in someone else's cloud. ~ Maya Angelou

Effective communications are those that bring in positive results. This can be done if you follow four simple tips:

1) Communicate in a way that leads to positive outcomes. Always assume positive intent from the person you are communicating with.

2) Even the harshest feedback can and should be delivered in a positive, supportive, team-centric "we" way.

3) Stay focused on the issue or behavior and not on the person's character.

4) Be kind and respectful. Always.

This week:

Pay attention to the words you use. Do they tend to be generally more positive or negative?

TIP #40: Show gratitude.

One joy shatters a hundred griefs.
~ Chinese Proverb

Think of someone who has had an influence or made a significant difference in your life. Who are they? What do you remember about them?

Sharing your gratitude with someone is a powerful way to communicate your feelings. Don't wait until it's too late. Do it now.

Here are a few ideas for displaying gratitude in a tangible way.

- Write and send a thank you letter. Describe the other person's qualities that had an impact on your life, such as courage, loyalty, support, kindness, wit, or persistence.

- Call or visit someone and thank them for being an influence on your life.

- Give a note to someone for no special reason. Say something like "I'm glad you are my son," "I'm glad you are here," or "your smile made my day."

You may be surprised at how powerful the experience of sharing gratitude can be.

This week:

Pick a way to show gratitude to someone who has made a difference in your life. Follow through. How did that feel?

TIP #41: Make a promise to yourself.

Knowledge is learning something every day.
Wisdom is letting go of something every day. ~ Zen Proverb

We all have things we wish we could do better, especially in the area of building and using better communication skills. Often, it's easier to learn about what you need to do than to actually do it.

How many times have you told yourself that you are going to listen more and talk less, but then sort of forget about it as soon as you have something to say?

Try making a promise to yourself.

- Write down you want to focus on changing or reinforcing in yourself on 3x5 cards. **You can cut the cards in half or quarters, depending on where you are going to store them.**

  Some of the promises I have written are listen, focus on one thing at a time, and be thankful.

- Find a small box that isn't serving a good purpose and put the cards in that box. Put the box somewhere where you'll see it first thing in the morning.

- Each morning pull one card and say "Today I will..." and read the card. Then focus on working on that promise all day. Carry the card with you in your bag, your notebook, your pocket.

- At the end of the day put the card back in the bottom of the pile. When you finish the stack of cards, reshuffle and start over.

This week:

Pick out a few communication tips you want to continue working on or review. Write down at least three that you want to focus on this week. What are your promises to yourself?

TIP #42: Connect with laughter.

Be sincere; be brief; be seated. ~ Franklin D. Roosevelt

Playful communication is a great way to draw others to you. When you laugh with someone, a positive bond is created. This bond can even act as a buffer against future disagreements.

Playful communication helps you:

- **Connect to others** - Laughter attracts and binds people together.

- **Smooth over differences** - Using gentle humor often helps you broach sensitive subjects, resolve disagreements, and reframe problems.

- **Overcome problems and setbacks -** A sense of humor is the key to resilience. It helps you take hardships in stride, weather disappointment, and bounce back from adversity and loss.

- **Put things into perspective** - Most situations are not as bleak as they appear to be when looked at from a playful and humorous point of view.

- **Be more creative -** Humor and playfulness can loosen you up, energize your thinking, and inspire creative problem solving.

Best of all, laughter is contagious—just hearing laughter primes your brain to smile and join in on the fun.

An important note: Always use *appropriate* humor. Stay away from anything that slightly resembles a sarcastic or derogatory remark. That can backfire. You never know what sensitivities the listener has.

This week:

Don't take yourself so seriously. What can you do to practice playful communication?

TIP #43: Look up.

Appreciate everything your associates do for the business. Nothing else can quite substitute for a few well-chosen, well-timed, sincere words of praise. They're absolutely free and worth a fortune. ~ Sam Walton

Do you tend to get so engrossed in what you are doing that you don't notice what's going on around you? Here's a really simple communication tip that will make a big difference in your relationships.

Look up.

Pay attention to what is going on around you. Consciously notice the little things that are going well and say something about them.

The things that seem small or insignificant to you can be a really big deal to someone else. Maybe it's new glasses, a new haircut, an engagement ring, or a smiling face.

Showing that you notice the small details by making a positive comment is a huge connector.

This week:

Do you tend to be into your own thing and not notice the small things going on around you? Practice looking up.

TIP #44: Share good gossip.

The least movement is of importance to all nature.
The entire ocean is affected by a pebble. ~ Blaise Pascal

Gossip can be hurtful and create an environment that will impede good communication. It can cause people to take sides, distort the truth, and show an overarching lack of respect.

Instead, spread some positive gossip.

When you hear something good about someone, tell someone else. If you hear someone did a good job at work, tell their boss. Don't you wish someone would do that for you?

Give affirmation to someone by appreciating them in the presence of others. Some people don't want to be acknowledged in front of a large group, but most people will be touched by being appreciated in front of someone else. Even something as simple as "You did a great job".

Sharing good gossip sets the stage for positive communication.

This week:

Tell someone you appreciate them in front of others. For example, tell your partner you are thankful for him in front of the kids or acknowledge someone's work in a staff meeting.

TIP #45: Tailor to your audience.

If you have nothing to say, say nothing. ~ Mark Twain

Communicating with your boss, co-worker, customer or family may require a slightly different communication style.
It's important to tailor what you need to say to who you are talking to.

- With your boss, be careful to pick the right time and ask for what you need and what he or she expects within a specific timeframe.

- With a co-worker, be direct, transparent, and open-minded.

- With a customer, listen carefully. Apologize if necessary even if it wasn't your fault and offer a solution.

- At home, don't take anyone for granted. Recognize the different relationships you have with your spouse, child, extended family, and friends.

Think about who your audience is and communicate with them accordingly.

This week:

Think about who you are talking to. How do you need to adjust for the different people you work and live with and perspectives they have?

TIP #46: Be open to the real truth.

Never apologize for showing feeling. When you do so, you apologize for the truth.
~ Benjamin Disraeli, Author

To communicate in an authentic way, you must be willing to look for the real truth.

When people share their stories with you, there are three truths to consider:

    1) Your truth
    2) Their truth,

And somewhere in between is

    3) **The truth**.

Tell your truth - sooner.

Many people have difficulty telling their truth about issues in a timely, direct, and caring way. When you tell your truth, as you know it, you will simplify the communication process and take the guesswork out of your relationships.

Listen openly to their truth – "tell me more"

Use your listening skills to hear what the other side of the story may be. Truly listen.
Then, think about both perspectives and talk about what the real truth may be. Usually it's somewhere in the middle.

This week:

Practice being authentic by speaking your truth and being open to listening to someone else's truth. Then look for what may be the real truth. How does that change your perspective on the situation?

TIP #47: It is what it is.

Yes, I sometimes fail, but at least I'm willing to experiment. ~ Bono

We all have a bad day now and then. When we do, sometimes it makes us behave badly. Maybe, something is going on in our lives that is overshadowing everything else. Maybe, we are in a personal crisis.

It happens to all of us.

It's important when you are communicating to realize that we all have complicated lives. If someone is having a bad day, you may need to just give them some grace.

When someone says or does something they shouldn't have or behaves in a way that is different than what you expected from them, ask yourself: Why would a reasonable person behave that way?

Then, before you react, ask. Is there something going on that I should know about? Maybe, they are going through a rough time.

Sometimes, letting it go and giving some space is the best way to respond. Then, you only address the issue or behavior only if it continues.

Sometimes it is what it is.

This week:

Be aware of what's going on in people's lives that may cause them to respond or behave differently. Is there someone in your life you may need to give some grace to this week?

TIP #48: Be a good role model.

You can't lead anyone else further than you have gone yourself.
~ Gene Mauch

One of the best ways to get good communication from others is to model it yourself. People will follow your lead if you are positive, consistent and display confidence.

- A good role model is someone people can look up to for guidance. They are trustworthy, respect others, and communicate positively.

- A good role model does what she says, delivers on promises, and can always be counted on. They demonstrate in their actions what others can do.

- A good role model doesn't blame. They set an example.

Are you a good role model?

This week:

Assess how good of a role model you are. Are you consistent in modeling good communication skills? How can you do better at modeling to others as to what you want from them?

.

TIP #49: Leave old baggage behind.

Leave your old baggage behind; the less you carry the further you go.

It's easy to carry around old baggage when we communicate with someone, especially someone you know fairly well. Bringing old complaints and issues into what is happening right now will get in the way of good communication.

When you are talking with someone about an issue, especially a sensitive one, make sure you leave old issues and experiences behind. Let it go and start fresh. Today.

Honestly seek to understand other viewpoints in the here and now. Don't compare to the past and don't drag in old issues.

Steps to leaving baggage behind:
- Stay in the moment.
- Keep the issue focused on what is happening right now.
- Don't attach old baggage to today's issue.

Letting go of old baggage in a relationship can be transforming. Allow yourself to start fresh. Share that you want to keep the discussion to the issue at hand and ask them to do the same. Be careful not to backslide into old habits. The more you can hone this skill, the more productive and satisfying your relationships will be.

This week:

Assess your relationships. Do you have anyone in your life that you tend to bring old issues into current situations?

TIP #50: Take baby steps.

We must not, in trying to think about how we can make a big difference, ignore the small daily differences we can make which, over time, add up to big differences that we often cannot foresee. ~ Marian Wright Edelman

Whatever you do, don't give up. Don't feel overwhelmed by what you want to work on. Chunk it down into baby steps. Practice each baby step until you are really comfortable. Then move on to a next step.

One small step each day will keep you moving toward your goal and on to your success.

This week:

Look over your notes so far and decide which baby steps you want to work on.

Write down one small step that you will take this week.

TIP #51: Reassess your skills.

You can't hit a target you can't see, and you can't see a target you don't have. ~
Zig Ziglar

Let's evaluate where you are since you started these lessons.
Answer *true* or *false*:

1. I listen more than I talk.

2. I speak specifically and personally, instead of generally and abstractly.

3. My body language corresponds with my words and my tone.

4. I check my tone (especially in written communication) to make sure it corresponds with my message.

5. I pay attention to one person/conversation at a time.

6. I don't rely primarily on written (e-mail and text) conversations.

7. I am clear in what I am saying and in sharing my expectations with others.

8. I make it comfortable or "safe" for others to talk to me about sensitive subjects.

9. I never avoid certain people or conversations. I tackle the hard conversations with ease.

10. I deal with issues as soon as they come up.

How does this compare to when you first took the assessment (Tip #1)?

This week:

What communication skills are you already doing well?

What would you like to continue to work on?

What's your plan for continuing to build on your communication skills? Goals that are written down are achieved 80% more often than those that aren't.

Write your goals down.

TIP #52: Every situation is brand-new.

If you hear a voice within you say 'you cannot paint,' then by all means paint, and that voice will be silenced. ~ Vincent Van Gogh

This is the last lesson and a very important one.

Continue to work on the areas you need to work on. By now, you should know what those are and have started working on improvement.

Here are some tips to your continued success:

- Respond and react differently. Rather than responding to a situation in an unconscious and automatic way, respond in a conscious and accountable way. Treat every situation as a brand new one.

- If you approach a situation or respond in a new way and it doesn't go so well, try again. If that approach doesn't work, then try a new one.

If it works do more of it. If it doesn't, then try something new!

- If necessary, ask for a "Do-over." Say you're sorry and restart the conversation over in a different way. Try a new approach until you find one that works. In close relationships, you may even want to agree to a "Do-over" clause. When things aren't going well, shout, "Do-over!" and agree that that is okay. It can help a stressful conversation from spiraling out of control

- Treat every situation as if it's the first time you have dealt with it. Then, deal with it in a brand-new way.

This Week:

Take some time to think about what you can do differently to get a different result. **Do you have a relationship that needs a "Do-over" clause?**

Conclusion

Congratulations on investing the time and energy in improving your relationships by developing better communication skills.

You have probably found that some of these tips hit home and others not so much. Make it a point to use the ones that work for you. Put them in your communication tool box. Practice them. Use them. Get comfortable with them.

The results will be transforming.

Continue your Learning

For more information resources and communication tips, visit www.cornerstone-ct.com

To schedule an individual consultation, coaching session, workshop, or training contact betty@cornerstone-ct.com

Ordering Information

This publication can be ordered direct from:
betty@cornerstone-ct.com

Quantity sales: special discounts are available on quantity purchases by organizations, associations, colleges and other groups.

52 Communication Tips is also available on Amazon.

ISBN-13: 978-1986822602
ISBN-10:1986822605

Courage is what it takes to stand up and speak;
Courage is also what it takes to sit down and listen.
~ Sir Winston Churchill

Made in the USA
Columbia, SC
22 May 2018